No Rhyme or Reason
Just Thoughts for the Season

Demetra "Lyrically" Adams

No Rhyme or Reason, Just Thoughts for the Season

Copyright © 2023 by Demetra "Lyrically" Adams

All rights reserved. No part of this publication may be reproduced, stored in a retrieval system, or transmitted, in any form or by any means electronic, mechanical, photocopying, recording, or otherwise, without the prior written permission of the author except in the case of brief quotations embodied in critical articles and reviews.

ISBN 978-1-949402-17-9

Cover Design: Donna Osborn Clark at CreationsByDonna@gmail.com

Layout and Interior Design: CreationsByDonna@gmail.com

Published by: Hummingbird and Yellow Rose Production
www.HummingbirdandYellowRose.com

Printed in the United States of America.

Dedication

This book is dedicated to Mr. Willie G. Adams, I. An American Hero, a United States Army and Vietnam War Veteran, lover of westerns, 60's and 70's soul, Fedoras, and his children, grandchildren, and great grandsons.

To me, you are Dad. You are missed. You are loved.

No Rhyme or Reason, Just Thoughts for the Season

In her first poetry book "No Reason or Rhyme, just thoughts over Time" Adams took several poems written from her school years through her thirties and put those into one book – truly "over time".

In "No Rhyme or Reason – Just Thoughts for the Season", Adams comes back with her pen, and uses it to respond to the "season" at hand. The current events, racial tension, senseless deaths, and support of Black Lives Matter – all while sprinkling the love for her God throughout.

She uses unique cadence, beats, and rhythms. Very creative and definitely worth the read. You may not agree with Lyric's words; she is not looking for agreement. Reading these poems is just an expansion of your own library of opinions, ideas, and truths.

In Memory

In this book I have written 4 poems dedicated to beautiful souls lost at the hands of those sworn to protect. I did not mention names because I did not have the specific permission to mention those names. I did try to reach out. Instead, I put the date of the tragic loss in the hopes that I would bring honor to them and remembrance.

For those lives lost to police violence:

10/20/2014 – 16 Shots
03/13/2020 – Shhh
05/25/2020 – Who Am I?
01/07/2023 – Mirror, Mirror

For those lives lost to senseless violence without provocation:

05/24/2022 - Mass Shooter   Uvalde School Shooting
09/04/2022 – Why, that day?   Saskatchewan Stabbings

In these reflections, it is not and was never the intention to offend family members or friends of those affected by these tragedies. These are solely and implicitly feelings and emotions that came about from the pain, rage, and tears shed by the author herself as she personally felt and dealt with the needless loss of life, too soon, that shook so many of us to the very core.

Please, receive these words in the spirit in which they are intended. My heart can not hide the pure agony it feels. It is exposed by the loud moaning, in painful concert with those left to grieve: families, friends, communities, and entire racial, cultural, and ethic groups tortured in kind.

Table of Contents

Black History Month 1

Chains on My Neck 7

16 shots (In Memory 10/20/2014) 12

Do not let your story be their glory 15

Mass Shooter (In Memory 05/24/2022) 23

My Head 26

Sunrise 27

Give America Back to God II 31

Why not inspire? 34

Legacy in Me 37

The Hope 40

Portrait of Woman By S. Rupsha Mitra 43

BEAUTY 46

What would you say? 48

Depression 50

Hallelujah 54

Shhhh (In Memory 3/13/2020) 56

Relax (A Fiction...Or is it?) 61

Row, Whip, Chase, Bang 65

Shadow 68

In Your Eyes 73

Little Brown Feet 76

Solitary Minds 81

Come to Me (Psalm 18)	83
Status Quo	86
And then you change…	88
Legacy	93
Stolen	94
What Say You?? A story of legality	96
PAIN	103
Who Am I?? (In Memory 05/25/2020)	106
Mirror, Mirror (In Memory 01/07/2023)	108
Heading towards Loss	114
The Day the Mountain Fell	116
Epilogue	121
Thank you for the Words	122

Black History Month

Celebrate Us!

Black
Outside the Box
Doing what no one expects

Black
Afro, Dreads, or Locs
Disregard us
You would regret

Bet!

Black, degrees
Black, making cheese
Yes, we do that
You disagree?

Have us in your life
A King
A Queen

You need a friend
We are no absentee

You need a prayer
We fall on our knees

You need to cry
We have a shoulder
For you to lean

Black people love
It's not just routine

Demetra "Lyrically" Adams

We talk trash
Yes, we can be obscene

But it doesn't stop there
We can also get clean

We
Rise Up
Jive Up
Laugh a lot
Then we
Tidy up

Black, wealth
We are building
Black, legacy

Movin' on up
Like George and Wheezy

Oh yes, indeed
See

Piece of the pie
Shit, we greedy!

Beauty
Intelligence
Entrepreneurial Success

Black History Month
The shortest month?
We could care less

Don't want you to feel
You've given us excess

Because Black History
Is really 12 months strong

No Rhyme or Reason, Just Thoughts for the Season

12 months long
Don't get me wrong

We are grateful
For the time
To celebrate us
In unity

But Black History Month
Is every day to me

Black is the New Black

You didn't think I was going to switch that?
Nah man
Keep that

When you're the best
You don't sweep that

Or creep that
You go to the mountain
Go steep with that

I'm Black and I'm Proud
Repeat with that

How deep is that?

It's a fact

Black, 365
Peep that!

You don't change from the best
Why digress
Lean in
Puff out your chest

Demetra "Lyrically" Adams

Set the mold
No regress

Black
Black
Black
Black

Don't you love
Just saying that?

Black neighbor
Mother, Brother
Father, Sister
Cousin, Friend

Let's turn up
Family

Black History Month
Celebration Begins!

No Rhyme or Reason, Just Thoughts for the Season

Demetra "Lyrically" Adams

No Rhyme or Reason, Just Thoughts for the Season

Chains on My Neck

She hangs her head
Her head down low
As people pass
They think they know

Those earrings are too heavy, too big
No, it's the weight of that high afro

That keeps her with her
Neck bent low

She sees them stare
Knowing their thoughts
It's not surprising to her
Many times, those looks she has caught

The supposition
The assumption
The stereotypical notion

Thinking they know
The cause of her
Head motion

It's an emotion

My earrings are not heavy
If they were, just like you
I would not wear them
I do because they are cute!

My Afro is my crown
It never weighs my head down

Demetra "Lyrically" Adams

My neck is bent because of all the suffering
At the hand of those who receive only buffering

While working, I receive only the latest shifts
To allow others to get home to their kids
I have kids…

I pay my bills
Always on time
And yet they find a reason
Some reason to add a fine

I'm educated
But you will never know
Because you won't talk to me
Because of my Afro

My clothes offend you
The colors of my motherland
Then you should have left us
 In that other land

Do you know I was actually told
Slavery might have been "bad"
But we know we are better off
Now owning things
We never would have had

Are you (pardon me)
Fucking kidding me?

They raped, sold, and beat us unmercifully?

Tearing our families apart
Mothers with full breast
For babies they would never get to hold
Never feel on their chest

No Rhyme or Reason, Just Thoughts for the Season

Better off?
Surely you jest

Whipped our backs
Like we could not feel
To care for their kids
Their homes
The cotton in their fields

We still get beat in the street
Paid on a different scale
Treated with indifference
What's the difference?

We're just not standing on a block for sale

Placing the change on the counter
Not in our hand

Grab your purse
Cross the street
Next to us you won't stand

I don't want your purse, Ma'am.

Walking on the backs of our ancestors
For a nice car or a cell phone?

Get away from me man!
That makes no sense
You know it's wrong!

Admit it's wrong!

Your words are a chain around my neck
No respect
No accountability
I interject

Back to my head being bent
And the people staring at me

You ever think that I look down
Your faces not to see?
The chains around my neck
That's what you are to me
Daily I seek the key
To unlock me, all of me

Grace and mercy
Please keep me free

As I walk
Inside I listen to a groovy beat
I watch my beautiful feet
While your faces, I choose not to see

Socialized negativity
Entangled and entwined
With racist acceptability

Nope, that shit ain't for me

Manipulating the legal system to keep us in for weed
When others commit murder and yet they get to walk free
Yes, the chains about my neck, some days it gets harder
But daily grace and mercy keep my strides from faltering

Don't be sad for me
Never that!
Because this is true
I'm about to offend some people
I hope it's not you

But I have my God
That hope that lies within
Yes, I cursed and said God in the same poem
And will probably do it again

No Rhyme or Reason, Just Thoughts for the Season

My God, My God
He died to set me free
Retrieved the keys to hell and death
And that is not just theoretically

Ruminate with me
For a second
Two or three

The hell on earth that many try to inflict
It does not work on me

Yes, my neck may be bent
But I'm saved, sanctified
And I've been set free!

CLICK!
Hear that?
Always

Grace and mercy
Grace and mercy
Grace and mercy

Releasing me

16 shots (In Memory 10/20/2014)

16 Shots
Rang out for 16 blocks
The smoke from every shot
Hung in the air like fog

Walking away
That's not the story they gave
For their own skin they wanted to save
Who cared who would lay in the grave?

We cared
And we still do
People rose up
Demanded the truth

It was not as you expressed
Feared for your life
Shaking in your vest

He was a child
No threat received
That very first shot
Knocked him off his knees

Why the rest
Why take the other 15 shots?
Because you can
You are a cop

Thus, we are left wondering
Who protects, and who serves
And who takes those extra shots
Because they feel we deserve

No Rhyme or Reason, Just Thoughts for the Season

The lesser end of their protection
As they know it's up to their perception
If for their safety, they say they fear
16 shots, you just might hear.

No Rhyme or Reason, Just Thoughts for the Season

Do not let your story be their glory

As you march in protest
Try to do your best

To hold your head up high
No one else must die

I walk with you
Shoulder to shoulder as you stand

Believing that freedom is a right
For every color man

Shout your message loud and clear
Black men and women matter

We have a right to be here

You give "white" reasons
To shoot us in the back

Holding black down
  "I can't breathe"

We know you heard that

A repeat melody of the air we lack
The air you take

 For that, you have developed a knack

Do not let your story be their glory.

Black wants to attack
Who cares about glory

Demetra "Lyrically" Adams

No Rhyme or Reason, Just Thoughts for the Season

We've got something for you right here
Come on…peep that!

But no, calm down
Deep breath
In
Out
Not strapped

Do it again

Exhale
Pause
Count to 10

Look at the big picture
Three-hundred sixty degrees
Don't let them win

They want us to cut up
So they can cut us down

Cameras rolling
They want to see us clown

Don't let our story be their glory

Our mothers are crying
Black men please, please stop dying

Going to jail for life
Think that's not death?

It's life, resigned

Walk to a beat like you are hearing drums
Singing the songs that our ancestors sung

Marching, moving our feet

While chanting

Black lives matter
There is no recanting

Don't make sudden moves
They will take up their guns

Expect that response
Don't you dare run

Stay en masse
Even when they bring out the gas

Let our first message
Also be our last

Stop killing our people
We deserve to breathe air

Our mothers are crying
Because their children are dying

Black people matter
And we deserve to be here

Stop watering down our message
Let the words ring clear

BLACK LIVES MATTER

Don't let your story be their glory

Stay on guard
Sons
Daughters
Beware the fraud

Let the fire that you carry

No Rhyme or Reason, Just Thoughts for the Season

Turn into a fire in your belly
No longer burn your own neighborhoods down
There is no retribution in that to be found

Although it gets the world's attention
The world will only mention

Thugs, hoods, and gangsters see
And the anger in you and me

Damn straight we are angry
We have every right to be

But don't burn up the streets
Or make it more bloody

We pound our own chests in agony
As we listen to our mother's pleas

Every tear drop that she releases

From *fear* of loss
Or for those already deceased

Do not let your story be their glory
Don't let them take anything else from you and me

Do not give them ammunition
Repeating "They just won't listen"

We are ready to hear
We are ready to be heard

Black lives matter
Our continuous words

Let your story be of a people who marched
With dignity, not with enmity

Demetra "Lyrically" Adams

Are you hearing me?

That gives them glory
And that is not our story

But for our lives, our very freedom, to exist and to stand
Shoulder to shoulder next to any color man.

How long are we expected to not RISE UP in anger
When we know our sons and daughters are in imminent danger?

Rise up now
Kings and Queens

And be aware that your sufferings
Yes, they will continue
But let's choose how we fight

And know that if we do this right
While we are in the limelight

Our people do not let them get glory
While we are living our story

Making history
Of this mystery

Of why a Black man can get shot
And his killer can go free

Repeatedly.

No Rhyme or Reason, Just Thoughts for the Season

Demetra "Lyrically" Adams

No Rhyme or Reason, Just Thoughts for the Season

Mass Shooter   (In Memory 05/24/2022)

I wake up early
Dress all in Black
Tie my combat boots
Prepare for my attack

I take my time
Walking to my prey
They have no idea
What's going to happen today

Before I get there
To that fateful place
Let me describe them
Each fated face

Children, ages unknown to me
Because I know not one of them, you see

Grandmothers, mothers, uncles, fathers
All who chose to be
Teachers, in addition to their role
On their family tree

Unselfish, sharing their knowledge
Manners, arts, character gifts from inside
Pouring into sweet children
Their little lives, aiming to guide

I choose not to see this
As I move at my own pace and stare
At people who are irrelevant
And soon will not be there

Demetra "Lyrically" Adams

I hold so much power and control
A "mass shooter" the public will soon behold
My name will go down in history
Although it will be for infamy

It matters not the reason why
It matters not if I live or die
So many will come after me
Mass shooter, that's our legacy

Shrouded with a long black coat,
combat boots
No legitimate reason in tote

My AR-15
Feels light as a feather
As I tiptoe to my new forever…BANG!

Mass shooter
As you wake up and plan
This horrible assault against your fellow man

I want you to know you do not win
You can't break man's spirit like you think you can

These little ones
Faceless and nameless to you
But I knew them before they even grew

In their mother's wombs
When I placed them there
They are special to me, so how do you dare?

These women and men, going about their day
Why do you think it's okay to take them away?
These people do not belong to you
No matter what you feel you have the power to do

No Rhyme or Reason, Just Thoughts for the Season

You lace your boots
Put on your black coat
Carry your AR15
Bad attitude in tote

You may shoot their body
But their soul you cannot touch Man, woman, boy, girl
Each now in an angel's clutch

You tiptoe in this world
This is where the devil roams
Do not be deceived
This is not my children's home

Mass shooter you want to go
Down in history
History has already been written
There is no mystery

You conniving killer
Nefarious, and yet you applaud
Don't speak so highly of yourself

You still must face your God!

My Head

Have you ever been in a state of mind
Where the weight of your mind
Is like a freight on your mind

Where the crates are stacked and packed
On pallets, it feels like mallets
Pounding, the sound is resounding
Oh my God, it's astounding that my head can tolerate this much
POUNDING

Why this internal pounding
Is it stress
Am I sleeping less
Emotions I'm trying to suppress

Lord, my head is a big mess

Your eyes are open
My tears pour like rain
Trying to make sense of all this pain
Is my head extensible?
Is that comprehensible?

Now the crux of the weight
Is the very state that I debate
Wanting to know if you relate
To the pain that I commiserate

I wipe my face
I grab my head
I lay back down
And go back to bed

But my head….

Sunrise

I rise every morning
To Thank God for the day
Never taking it for granted
One day, it won't be this way

So, while I am yet able
To see the sunrise so bright
I will rejoice and be glad in this day

The sky, Your canvas, and my delight!

Psalm 119:164
Seven times a day
I praise Thee, Lord

The sun begins to peak the sky
The colors changing by and by
From clouds of white and blue
To yellow, and orange so bright

The sun is in full glory
To my sheer delight

I never want to take for granted
The opportunity

To thank God for allowing
A beautiful sunrise
My eyes to see

Let me paint the picture
Of how this story could have been:

We could live in Black and White
No color anywhere

And without any knowledge of color
We would not even care

It would be like living as a shadow
Almost like not being there

No red roses
Purple pansies
Pink buttercups
Orange leaves
Green grasshoppers
Colorful parrots
Or rainbows…

No colors anywhere –
And we would not miss them at all.

But God loves us so much
And has endless creativity
That He not only gave us color
He gave it to us for FREE!

We see it in the sunrise
A different version every day

He didn't stop there
Not My God
Don't play!

The sunset is unique as well
Every night, a different romantic spell

No Rhyme or Reason, Just Thoughts for the Season

The birds, the trees, the types of grass
The fur on the animals too!

I could go on…

I tell you what
I had to take a Praise Pause (That's True!!)

So, yes, we could have lived

In Black and White

And never a sunrise missed

We would not have known to miss them

Because we would not have known the difference.

Thank God for the Sunrise

No Rhyme or Reason, Just Thoughts for the Season

Give America Back to God II

My country tis of thee
We cannot walk the streets
Sweet land of liberty
Schools under lock and key

For thee I pray

Land where our fathers died
What happened to our pride?

Danger on every side

Where is freedom's ring?

Father, you know where it went
Our knees have not been bent
Less time on You we have spent

Please hear our cry!

This country, I give back to Thee
It can all start with me
At night I'll bend my knees
So freedom can ring

I wrote this in 2008
Hoping America would change it's fate
Fallen from the world's pedestal, no longer great

Is freedom even a thing?

Men and women killed for peace
Soldiers now occupy the streets
Mothers praying that the violence would cease
Please hear our cry
Betsy Ross' flag

Demetra "Lyrically" Adams

Represents an entirely new meaning
Civil unrest and racial demeaning
No one seems to be retreating
All the while, hate is seething

America, for thee I pray

That you will soon see that this is not the way to be
Conflict, confusion, coercion, and complicity
Being on the side of them or on the side of we

No concern for the generations coming after me
The message that our youth can learn what they need
From the streets
Where is our humanity?

To battle with guns
Raise your voice, little ones
Learn to fight with your words
Get the government to hear you
That's a joke
But we can get our people to stay woke

Not woke in words
But work in spirit
Work in courage, can you hear it
Swing low, sweet chariot
Do you want to go home?

Is this our home?
America is our home
That's what freedom was built on
That's the fabric in which the flag was stitched
How our generations will be cultivated, how they will be enriched
Give America back to God
Make freedom a thing
Give meaning to the flag
Let our voices ring.

No Rhyme or Reason, Just Thoughts for the Season

Why not inspire?

Don't know what to do today?

Be inspiring
Do something new, incredible, AMAZING!
Always know that people, especially **little eyes**, have their eyes on you!

Be inspirational
You have a story
Tell it.

No one can write your story like you can
No one can live your story like you can
Do not try to copy someone else
They are, indeed, the perfect copy of themselves

You are the exact and perfect image of you.

Believe that

Be inspired
Read a book about someone or something that changed the arc of history.
Listen to a song that reminds you of a time in your life
A time that changed your life.

Rehearse a line in a poem, a verse in the Bible, or remember a quote
Your parents' wise words
My Mother used to always say "And this, too, shall pass"
I cannot count the number of times that simple phrase has kept me pushing forward Thank you, Mom.

No Rhyme or Reason, Just Thoughts for the Season

Inspire
Light a fire
To go higher
Can't quench that desire
It's a power
A drive
Yes, something I require

I see your smile
I know you admire

Aspire

To inspire

Yet, you expire
Retire
In mire

Too lazy to produce
Might make yourself perspire

And so you sit
Quit

Tired of it

Let someone else
Inspire

Now…that's just bleak and **dire**

Count me out
I'd rather inspire!

Legacy in Me

As I walk across this stage so proud
I hear the cheering of the crowd
And as I'm handed my degree
I see my family watching me

My ancestors sitting straight and tall
Some know me well, others not at all

It mattered not how much they poured into me
I was still their own, their legacy

Vivian, my grandmother
Beautiful smile so wide
Not always so
When as a child, she would appropriately chide

George, my grandfather
A genteel man
Always sliding quarters
In my hand

Although they have passed
Resting in God's presence
I do not forget
Or neglect
Their lessons

The legacy in me
Their lifelong blessing

But that's not all
Rosa Parks is here
She's sitting right up front
In the very first chair

Demetra "Lyrically" Adams

Martin Luther King Jr.
Holds a sign up in his hands
You are the dream I had
Now go and change the land

As I walked off the stage
Harriet Tubman greeted me
She whispered "Slavery is the next thing to hell"
Be mindful that your very mind
Does not turn into a bondage cell

Treat it well

W.E.B. Du Bois
Shook my hand, then knowledge he did give
"Your thoughts, your deeds, above all your dreams, still live."

I felt in my heart
He wanted me to fly on the wings of an eagle
This prolific man who created
The National Association for the Advancement of Colored People"

My face was now covered
With my tears
My mind releasing
Its earlier fears

My ancestors don't expect miracles
They just want me to exist and BE here

There is no pressure
To bring popularity
To bring fame

I do not have to garner
Grandeur to our name

I walked to my chair

No Rhyme or Reason, Just Thoughts for the Season

Sat down within the crowd
Thought to myself
"If they could see me now"

Those who paved the way
For Black to read and learn

Opening the door
A Master's degree to earn

I thank you for your courage
For the strength it took to be
John Chavis, in 1799
The first Black college student in American history

You have entrusted much to me
To carry on this legacy
Make an impact in this life
For those coming after me.

That is the legacy in me.

The Hope

I Peter 3:15

But sanctify the Lord God in your hearts: and be ready always to give an answer to every man that asketh you a reason of the hope that is in you with meekness and fear.

> I expect
> I desire
> And I believe it is real
>
> The joy
> The happiness
> This hope that I feel
>
> But what happens when the happiness is not quite there?
> Do I lose all hope, fall into despair?
>
> What good would that do
> As a witness to others?
>
> Showing disbelief
> Resignation
> To my sisters and brothers?
>
> When I know that my Lord
> His promises are true
>
> Any shake-up in my faith
> Well, I'm human too!
>
> So here I am ready
> Willing
> And able
> To stand

No Rhyme or Reason, Just Thoughts for the Season

Separated
Set a part
Designated for Your plan

Ready to give an answer
Of Your promises, true

That Jesus Christ
Came
Died
Rose again

For me
And for you.

That's the hope that lies within

That He's coming back too

Portrait of Woman
By S. Rupsha Mitra

It is difficult to portray Razia, Laxmi Bai, Ahilya, and all such names
In a frame, within few pages of history books
As a woman ruler, inspiration, *strong, independent* woman from times, eons, moments,
where they were
They *are*...
Still

Dwelling in the woods
Covered within palkis, burqas, Ghoonghats, Ondormohols

Being a woman Sultan in a man's world was never easy, quotes history books.
Dissected wildly, jammed, restricted, punctuated with the singularity of perspectives.
What is even this man's world?

How we cannot change our allusions, our terminologies, our severe differentiation?
Why is even Razia not celebrated for her emergence
 From the shackled intricate barriers of society?
Why is there tendency of this obnoxious comparison?
Why?
Mardaani is the word for women warriors who fought ravages of times.

How we have been closeting the shakti, the Srishti, the celebration of
 being a woman!
Sans the dampening geographies in comparison,
Sans the entrenched biases
This is an ode for the woman - for being woman
For realizing the Shakti for the power in being a woman!
For woman and woman and woman
For every woman

Ode to Thammam (my grandmother)
I remember, being an adolescent, discovering a photo subsiding in the cornered
Molten mayhem, greyed memoirs behind Sebeka jeweled almari doors.
And abruptly realizing how Grandmas are *women* too.
Ladies as they called themselves
With kajal aureoled like rimming secrets
Her swirling silvered Zari saree ravishing in an air of cold mystery
Somewhere that is hard to reach as she simmers stories
Stealthily allowing her fluid fingers –felicity
As she weaves the Safa silk jacket and furtively grins at me
Persuading, nagging teen
Wanting her to unfurl this debris
 Magical and gaudy yet beyond my imagining
Her fierce halo of freedom surpassing the silence.

Now I trace
how I have grown in the company of her communion
The paragon mind -body homeostasis how she has never let the chaotic burden
of stereotypes, gaps, synapses, distant deviations in generations
Snap the lilac link between us, how we have traversed spaces like kins
Like women, who are eternally
Friends

How she let the barriers break into extensity
Let her blessings fall upon me like dusk mantras,
How she held my hand tight when
The broken wreckages of grist, beaten love disintegrated
My self, she held me, hugged me every time I was broken
And whispered as she does till now with her ever greened smile and silvered hair

'Rupsha, tumi parbe, dekho jemon ami hat ta bariyechhi, ei prithibi o tar hat bariye achhe
, nijeo egiye jao tar haat ta dhoro,' (Rupsha. You can. See, how I have extended my hand, the universe too has its hand extended towards you. Take your step ahead and hold its hand)

S. Rupsha Mitra is a writer from India with a penchant for everything creative. Her works have been published in literary magazines such as: **London Reader, Mermaids Monthly, Pif Magazine, Birmingham Arts Journal, Muse India, Indian Literature (Sahitya Akademi), Science for the People Magazine**, and many more. Mitra has worked as an editor for Rasa Literary Review, been a script writer for an audio theatre, and continues to maintain her writing entries on her personal website: http://www.srupshapoetry.com/

She won a special mention in the eShe poetry contest and in 2022 was the first-place winner of the BLACC contest as sponsored by Gordavi, LLC. It was here that Mitra was noticed by the author of this book.

S. Rupsha Mitra's poetic submission: "Portrait of a Woman" is a powerful, cultural depiction of the beautiful, strong women in the Indian culture. This fell directly into what BLACC stands for: Building Legacy Artistry Community Culture. Her entry garnered her publication into this book, which is an honor to this author, as well as to the BLACC community.

BEAUTY

Beautiful
Essence
As
Unique
To
You

as

Breathing
Easy
Against
Unwrinkled
Tender
Years

Building
External
Acceptance
Uncanny
Togetherness
Yielding

To God
To self
To mindfulness

To voice

To choice

No Rhyme or Reason, Just Thoughts for the Season

To uncommon good

To unselfish brother and sisterhood

To self-made

B.E.A.U.T.Y.

Demetra "Lyrically" Adams

What would you say?

What would you say
If it were your final day
If you knew it were your last day to pray
Leave an impression for replay

What would you say?

I love you seems the obvious choice

But being obvious
Is not the obvious voice
Of course

Because we might lend some caution
Add more reason
Maybe a laugh
A memory of a season

I love you just might not be enough
Coming up with our last words
It's tough

What would you say?
On your final day

If you could choose your day
Typically, we don't get that say

A lot of choices we are granted
However, for most, we don't get that one to make

It works out okay
Well, I guess I can't say

No Rhyme or Reason, Just Thoughts for the Season

I haven't experienced that day
Thank God, I pray

What would I say…

I love you…I love you all and you will be okay.
Pull my finger! (You have to leave them with a smile)

I love you

Depression

Aggression
Obsession
You track me with pure possession

Who are you?

Depression.

Pushing
Pulling
No regression

Decompression
Release me, please
I shout in heated expression

Get away from me, Depression!

Tired, wanting
Demanding
Recession
Digression

Yet, you creep, crawl up my back
You know the direction

Aiming for my mind
Trying to overtake it with
Depression.

Whispering your indiscretions,
I mean MY indiscretions
Reiterating those to me
As if I am confessing

No Rhyme or Reason, Just Thoughts for the Season

My life lessons
Transgressions
Making me pause
To give reflection

On why I feel such a disconnection
from those around me
Is it them, or me that I question?

That's just the Depression.

See, it's my own misperceptions
Of my life
That make your mis-impressions seem right

Depression, you overtly slide me micro-expressions
Gently nudging my own neglections
Of my self-esteem
Slyly throwing constant misdirection

Shame on you, Depression.

You play with my inner-feelings
Like I'm a puppet on a string
Now requiring intercession
To my Father in heaven
Because He knows your predilection

Known to make me feel congestion
In my mind, full of your oppression
The center of my intellectual expression

Demetra "Lyrically" Adams

Yes, Depression, your cards have been shown.
The real deceptions

Unworthy

Unwise

Unloved

But you are wrong,

Depression.

I solider on
Repossessing
My mind
Confessing

No aggression, just concession
For the lessons that have been learned
While battling
Depression.

No Rhyme or Reason, Just Thoughts for the Season

Hallelujah

Why do we "Hallelujah" sing
Lift our hands our voices ring
Why do we "Hallelujah" shout
What exactly are we talking about?

Jesus, Jesus down in my soul
He makes those Hallelujahs roll
Out of my mouth
Down to my feet
Sometimes we can barely hold our seat

What has He done to deserve our song?
That list would be way too long
He's fed me
Clothed me
Woke me up today
He's led me
Directed me
Taught me what to say
So, I praise my Jesus
I hallelujah sing

To my Lord, God of everything

He sat with me when my Grandmother passed
Told me how she was running fast
Completely healed, no longer paralyzed
That sparkle in her big, dark eyes

Why do we hallelujah sing
To Christ the Almighty King
He could have called a legion of angels right away
To take Him off the cross, and kill them all that day

No Rhyme or Reason, Just Thoughts for the Season

He chose to stay upon that tree
To take those stripes that cut so deep
To wear the crown of thorns and bleed
He would have stayed there just for me

I bow my head in reverence due
I can never repay or fully thank You
But I lift my hands, my voice, my song
Singing Hallelujah to the Holy One

Why do we Hallelujah Sing
Because our God loves us above everything
He meets our needs, our battles won
Our deepest desire is to hear "Well Done"

Demetra "Lyrically" Adams

Shhhh (In Memory 3/13/2020)

Shhh, Quiet, Quiet Shhh,
Police on the ready

Geared up
Have warrant
Everyone steady

No knock needed
That was the plan
Everyone quiet
Guns in hand

Shhh…be quiet

Serve the warrant Nowhere to run

There's no retreating We have our guns

Hit the door
Did you hear that?
A bump in the night

We're starting to fret

Chill out guys
No one knows we are coming

It's dark
They are asleep

And…our guns will keep anyone from running.

Did something move?
Is someone stirring about?

No Rhyme or Reason, Just Thoughts for the Season

(Hell, maybe! I mean realistically, this is someone's house)

Since we're not sure

(Are we being too hasty?)
Nah, We're prepared
Everyone take off your safety

It doesn't matter
That we might startle
Cause a fright

Make someone
Jump out of their bed
In the middle of the night

We've got control of this situation
Besides; we are almost done…

Does everyone have their nerves in check?

Don't forget don't let them…

What was that?

Whatever happened to saying
"Stop! Police! Don't Run!"

Progress has deemed
We don't have to say that anymore
Precedent has shown
If we shoot first, it's okay
We still get to walk out of the courtroom door

We can empty our gun
And still go free
16 shots
Have gone into one teen
Who wasn't even running

Demetra "Lyrically" Adams

Police tried to hide the truth
Tragic shooting of this Black youth

For the amount of time that the police received
Yes, he truly might as well have gone free

One trauma at a time
Don't stack them - it's too many

Let's get back to this scene
Lord knows, there are plenty
Wait for the signal

Fire at will
We walked in
Woke up
And caused a fright

Yet we were the ones
Absolved of all wrong
For killing a 26-year old Black female
That night

No one feels guilty
As the cops plead their case
Who cries for this young lady?
For her mother
It's a disgrace.

Burying a daughter
Dreams that now lay in a grave
Goals and laughter
Covered by dirt

And the tears from her grieving Mother's face

Did anybody pay?

Her people were on FIRE and ready to FIGHT

No Rhyme or Reason, Just Thoughts for the Season

But even that could not make this situation right

What happens to the cops?
Did they lose their job?

Where is the justice for that dark night?
We march, we pray, we want made right.

We can't recover that night - it can't be made right.

Only time can heal what they have severed

What they took is gone forever.

What does "justice" say about that wicked night

 "Shhh! Quiet, quiet!"

We feared for our lives.

Standing in the position
WE put ourselves in
No one told us those stairs to walk up

No one told us to that door to NOT knock

"Shhh! Quiet, Quiet!"

Stop your lying…it's over played

You just wanted to kill a Black person
So that's what you did that day.

Demetra "Lyrically" Adams

No Rhyme or Reason, Just Thoughts for the Season

Relax (A Fiction...Or is it?)

Sit back and relax
But if you are Black
It's never time for that
So, we just tensely ease back

Watching
Ever diligently
No need to act
But ready to react

Looking over our shoulders
For that
Click Clack
What did we do?
Whiplash
A smack and a deep gash

Sir, may I ask…
No, you cannot ask
You keep talking and
I'll tear gas
Or trigger your Black ass

Now I hear clank clash
Got chains on me
Like an animal
Being led to a cage, I see

Eyes staring as I pass

Like something they've never seen
Knowing they do this everyday
To people that look like me

Demetra "Lyrically" Adams

It's like a game
We are not real people
Like we don't have family

As they relax
No pressure
No watching their back
Because they know better

It's their world and
Those are the facts

Shoot bang

This brother had a gun?
They did not carefully
Check this one?

Now Click Clack
My ass is done

But as I lay on the ground
Bullets circling all around
I want you to hear me speak

Their story will say
I had a gun, I tried to run away
But each person in that room
Knows what happened that day

Click Bang
My hands were in chains
There was no way I could shoot

My ankles were locked
I could barely walk
No way that I got loose

No Rhyme or Reason, Just Thoughts for the Season

Explain this to us
The people that look like me say
How did this happen
And the cops just walk away?

Sit back and relax
But if you are Black
It's never time for that
We keep our eyes up
Guard up
Stay up
Prayed up
Hell, stand up

Knowing the way systemic racism has moved up
The chain, the ladder
Dare I say hierarchy

Relax
Sit back
Nah
There is too much at stake for that.

Demetra "Lyrically" Adams

No Rhyme or Reason, Just Thoughts for the Season

Row, Whip, Chase, Bang

Row, whip, chase, bang

This is the song
That my people sing

Row

The high waves that brought us
Across the ocean against our will
Are the waves that also buried
Many of our dead and the our ill

While in the boat
Shackled ankles and hands
We rode, confused and perplexed
About the white man

Boats arrived at the shore of a land
That did not and does not want us still
We were now in a place
Where we had no free will

And the song we chant…remains still

Whip

We were no longer men
They beat our backs
Stole our children
Denied us land

We did their bidding
As they did their bedding
Of our wives and young girls

Demetra "Lyrically" Adams

Rape was a regular and accepted activity
We were helpless, just had to look on

Their whip had no preference
Just a demand for deference

Thank God for the underground
For the ones who became mentally strong
The people who rose up
Tired of being treated wrong

Row, whip, chase, bang

Now we are "free"
Men of intelligence and well-being

Highly educated, well-dressed
Full of hopes, full of dreams

Yet when we drive down the road
Here come the police

Scoping us stealthily
You think I don't see it?
But I have basic needs…

Their intentional pursuit
Of the Black man doing *"wrong"*
Going to work
Then going back home

Poignant questions like
Whose car is this?
Where are you going?

No Rhyme or Reason, Just Thoughts for the Season

Interesting, you allowed that
Speeding, White man to pass
Without knowing his answers to those questions
Man, "Kiss my ass!"
Chase

Of course, I said that in my head
If I move wrong, I'll end up dead

He's asking me to get out of my car
I don't know why he's asking that for
You can see I'm dressed for work
No weaving, no speeding
My Black skin is your torque

Chase

I know I have to listen
To an officer of the law
I open the door and get out of my car

Bang!

"He was aggressive" the officer said
That is why he ended up dead.

Row, Whip, Chase, Bang

The history of my people

Slain.

Shadow

Tall
Big
Black
Motionless

Captivating
Disappearing
Still
Small

Distorted
Contorted
Distended
Blended

Moving
Faster
Faster
Stop

Here
We
Go
Again....

Bouncing
Leaning
In-betweening

Short
Wide
Side to side

No Rhyme or Reason, Just Thoughts for the Season

Shadows
Lurking
Illuminating

Casting light
Fading
Shading

Why do you dance
Upon that wall?

Your funny movements
Jaunting
Suspicious
Hard to recall

All you've ever done
Is stalk me
Chase me
Taunt me

You freely come out in the sun
And bump right into everyone

But when the rain pours down from the sky
You scurry away
Occupied for the day

Our relationship, it seems one-sided
Which is very sad to me
You chose to come out when you please
Wouldn't you agree?

Lurking
Stalking
Interlocking

Shadow
Sometimes I think you are mocking

Demetra "Lyrically" Adams

Intermittent
Interlude
That truly sounds a little rude.

Shadow
Since I have no control
I cannot grab you
I cannot hold

I cannot call you to meet for a walk
You don't like the weather?
You surely will balk

The proximity
The gloom
The darkness
The lore

I grab my jacket
I peek out the door

Will my shadow
Lend me time to spend
For a walk?
Will he attend?

I close the door
Run down the stairs
My shadow meets me
He's standing right there!

Come on and follow me
My abstract friend

Transform
Translate
Transcend
Pretend!

No Rhyme or Reason, Just Thoughts for the Season

No Rhyme or Reason, Just Thoughts for the Season

In Your Eyes

I saw the cheating in your eyes
Before you verbalized your lies
I felt it - compromise
In my chest
That you had laid on another's breast

Do you deny
How long it's been
This assignation
With your "friend"

I felt the cheating
My heart, resigned
Your haunting, jaunting
Solo ride

No thought
Of my pain
Just of your pride

Controlled by lust
That touch, deep thrust
Pure lust

Just not us

So here I stand
Looking at "my" man

As he asks me to please
Just understand
What do I do
With this emptiness?
I beat my fists
Upon my empty chest
My guilt for not being everything you need

Demetra "Lyrically" Adams

Incapable of making our marriage succeed

I walk away
Take a breath
Then sigh

The hurt is real
I won't deny

But getting to this point I see
You really don't want to be with me

I pack my guilt
No longer want to feel
This useless emotion
Which my body steals

Get back up
No sitting still
Piece back together my pride
My will

I saw the cheating in your eyes
My heart could feel your hidden lies

Defiled our vows
threw out our rings

I'm done
I'm finished
With this hypocritical thing

Your choice was more important than me
More valuable than our hopes and our dreams
You invested in a mystery
When you had a very real me

You saw good-bye in my eyes

No Rhyme or Reason, Just Thoughts for the Season

Before I packed up and left
Went on with my life
You felt the loneliness in your chest
How quiet the silence can become
Pure stress
Loneliness can turn into
A palpable thing

That temporary fling
When you had the real thing

That fucking turned nothing
No real connection upon inspection
Cheating is not what you meant to do
Not getting caught is the real truth

I saw the cheating in your eyes
Now baby boy, no more – no more lies.

Little Brown Feet

Little brown feet
Walking through the house
Quietly searching
For the man you shot down

Little brown feet
Going to his room
Where is Daddy
Is he coming home soon?

Little brown feet
Eyelashes so long
She's dressed for her tea party
But Daddy isn't home

Dressed in her tutu
Tea kettle just right
Daddy promised we would play tea party
Isn't he coming home tonight?

Little brown feet
Searching, trekking all around
Not yet knowing
That the police shot you down

Whatever they are saying
Is leaving my MaMa in distress
If I were older I would tell them
To please, say less

And get away from my MaMa
Can you not see she is in agony
Where is my Dad?
He would stop this immediately
Little brown feet

No Rhyme or Reason, Just Thoughts for the Season

Looking at a picture of his kind-hearted Dad
This statuesque man
Would never let us be sad

Tonight, being a tall, built Black Man
Came back to haunt your Dad
The cops didn't care
About the little brown feet that he had

They didn't know that we throw the football
I'm learning to catch it just right
Nor did they know that you play tea party
With sister every Thursday night.

My Dad is coming to school with me
It's kindergarteners bring y our Dad's Day next week
He's also building a tree house for us
He called it man-cave; I felt so tough

Mom catches herself
When she sees me
She whispers "I will do this with dignity"
She sat me down
Looked in my eyes
"Tonight is the night that your Daddy died"

Let me explain
My perceptive little guy
Your Dad was shot helping someone
Because he could not just walk by

The cracking of her voice
Gave way to her resolve
MaMa called it grief
The pain, loss, and sheer disbelief

"I should not have asked for that milk
I should have let it be"

Demetra "Lyrically" Adams

Mom is still talking
But it was no longer to me
Little brown feet scurry away
As his mom repeats, "I should have gotten milk earlier in the day"

I should not have asked him to stop
I had time to go to the store today
I really just forgot
And that is why you got shot

A man was hitting his girlfriend
And you intervened
But the cops were sure you were the aggressor
As soon as they arrived at the scene

Pow, pow, pow
They raised their guns
Not caring about the little brown feet
Your daughter, your son

Leaving little brown feet
Feeling angry and cast aside
Trying to understand
The night their Daddy died

They will get it when they get older
These deaths making us colder yet bolder
Little brown feet
Push that anger away
Make your dad proud
Stay alive, okay?

Little brown feet
Transform into a big Black man
Be careful living this life
Do all the good you can
Remember your Dad
And what he valued, especially
Those little brown feet

No Rhyme or Reason, Just Thoughts for the Season

That he loved exceedingly

Let go of vengeance
Anger will tear your soul apart
But this cannot keep occurring
Innocent blood flowing
Knowing
Little brown feet – keep growing and growing

Showing
Ongoing
Fortitude

Being raised without their Daddy's
Knowing
It didn't have to be
This way

Maybe it will change one day
Little brown feet…

He didn't want to go away.

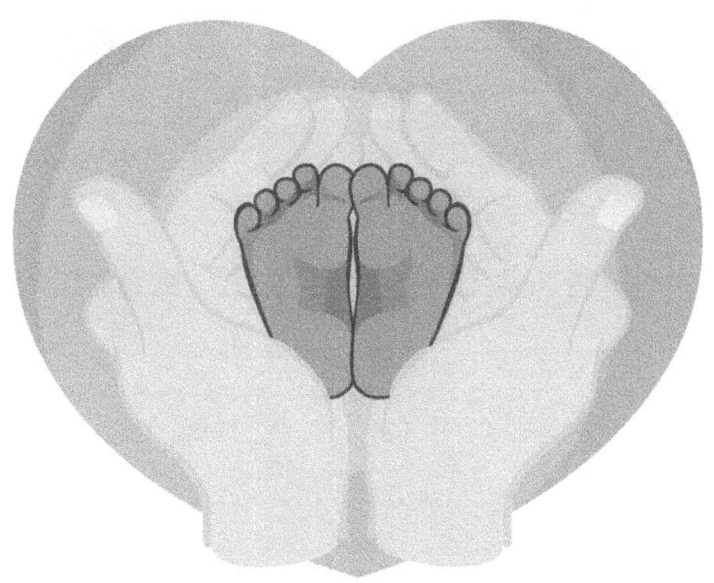

Demetra "Lyrically" Adams

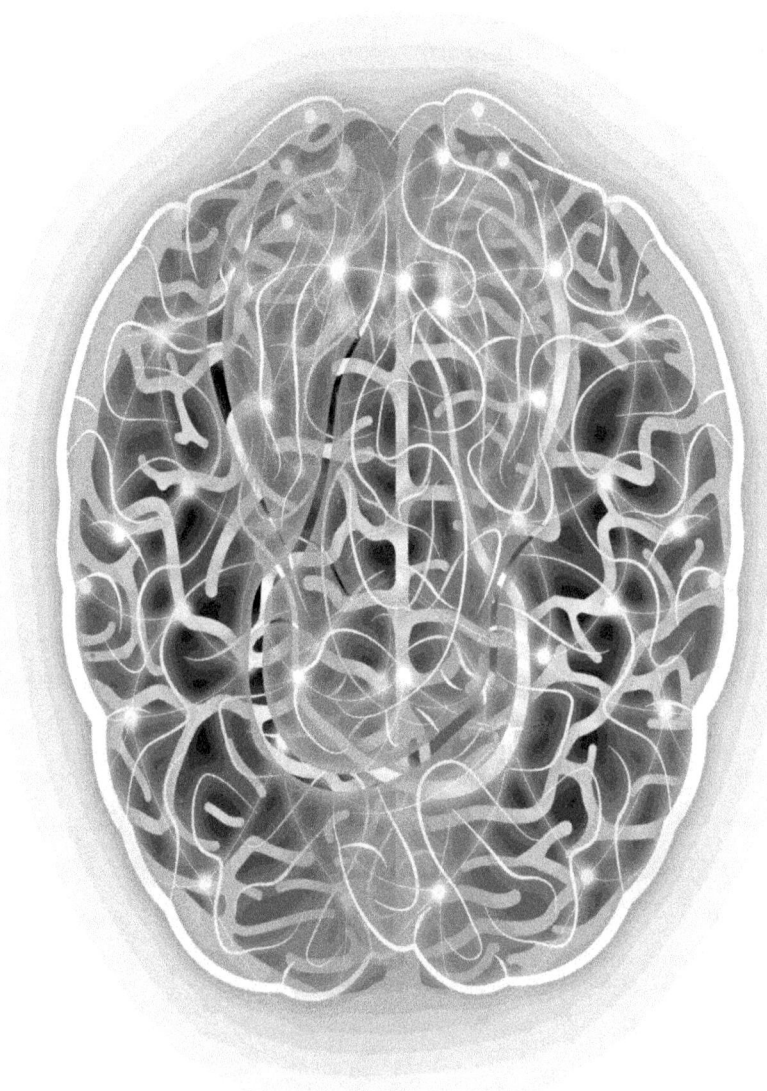

No Rhyme or Reason, Just Thoughts for the Season

Solitary Minds

Solitary minds
Take solitary time
To create
Associate
To relegate their conscious binds

And shake off what the world feels is so damn refined

No, my solitary mind is all mine
It's just fine
What is here, I've cultivated over time
Shaped, molded
And I call it divine

Don't aim to prevent my mind from showing its' shine
Oh, did you just get blinded by that last line?

My pitch, my flow
Is it causing you to become sublimed?
Vapors leaving your mind
As your thoughts become heated
Because I remain kind

My mind is not confined
To what you're inclined to see
I'm not in that box
That prison, wrapped in chains where you put me

My mind is free
My solitary mind
So divine
Never should you undermine
That strength, so intertwined

Demetra "Lyrically" Adams

In the cerebral cortex, cerebellum, hypothalamus
Thalamus, Pituitary Gland, Pineal gland, Amygdala
Hippocampus, and the Mid-brain
Because, you see

All those parts of the brain
Make up all the parts of me

My solitary mind
Is so well designed
So carefully enshrined
Not requiring anyone to cosign

On my thoughts
No, I'm just fine
Sitting here

Unencumbered
Unimpeded
Unrestricted
Unconditionally unbound
Undefeated

Freely unconstrained
Unabridged
You better believe it

So I reiterate
I'm fine
With my solitary mind

Encircling my body
Yes, I feel it

And I feel just fine

Come to Me (Psalm 18)

When I was just a little girl
All caught up in my little world
There were times when I would get so sad
Not understand that "life's not so bad"

I'd run and fall
I'd scrap my knee
My Mom would sweet and gently
Whisper, baby come to me

I've got you, baby come to me

Oh, the good those words would do
The many things they got me through
My Mother's voice, her whispered decree
Always saying "Come to me"

She'd wipe my tears
She'd tend my wounds
The same stayed true even as I grew
But she would never tell me what to do

Her words were always
This too shall pass
Make sure your questions, to Jesus ask

Dear God
In my solemn state, I query
Please don't hesitate, as I feel so weary
Please say those magic words I crave
The words, so many times, that saved

Me from hurt, anxiety, despair
Because I knew there was someone there
Now, Adonai, I lean on thee
I'm waiting, Master, say "Come to me"

Demetra "Lyrically" Adams

Come all you who are heavy laden
And I will give you rest
As long as this trial lasts
In the shadow of my wing
 Under the covering of my breast

Oh yes, My child, you can come to Me
Because I hear your open plea

In your distress
I know your voice
In spite of your fears
You make a joyful noise

I hear your cry; it comes to Me
Before My ears, your beautiful decree
I feel you, My child
And on your behalf

I shake the earth
I make it tremble
Under My very grasp

I let your enemies know
You are MY child
I will thunder from heaven
Hailstones and coals of fire

Scattered arrows
Your enemies will run and cower
They will all feel
My protective power

Why do I do these things?
Why do I deliver you when you come to Me?
Because I delight in you
To such a great degree

No Rhyme or Reason, Just Thoughts for the Season

Come to me, My child
I can protect you from it all
Those who trust in Me
Can run through a troop
They can leap over a wall

Sorrows encompassed me
Distresses fell, to my dismay
But in the day of calamity
You were there, Lord, to save the day

He asked me to walk uprightly
After His righteousness
My life I am to model

Lord, I thank you for being here
Your love for me to see
Like the comfort of my Mom's words: "This too shall pass"
Your precious words are "Come to me"

Status Quo

Perpetuating the status quo
Is not a status, bro
That we want to know
As we continue to grow

Can you hear me, though?

See, status quo
That means to be content
Not rocking the ship
Staying the same
Moving at a very slow clip

That is not my thing
I've got too much to bring
Identifying, yes, within me similarities
And likenesses that do not mean bland
But a combination of which mean BANG!

Did you hear that?
Boombambastic!
Hell yeah
My status is fantastic

When I walk, I sway
Nothing plain about my gait
When I talk, I have a twang
Yep, my voice has its own original slang

When I write, I lean on my desk and smile
Knowing my rhythm has its own resemblant style
Perpetuating the status quo
Sis, that can't be my status though

No Rhyme or Reason, Just Thoughts for the Season

I shake things up
I rock, then I roll
Tie up
Loosen
Am secretive
Translucent

Status quo?
That's not my status, No!
Never been my status, Yo

I create, debate
Relate or commiserate
Shake the dust off
Get back up
Love my "beau"
Make that dough
But never, not ever
Do I perpetuate
The status quo.

And then you change...

Joy, fear, excitement and overwhelming calm
Some of the emotions I felt
When I knew I was going to be a Mom
My first thought "I barely know how to take care of myself"
And without question, I must soon care for someone else

It was then that I changed

Altering the perspective of how I viewed myself
Was a priority as I struggled with self-esteem
Self-value, self-wealth

Positive and uplifting adjectives
Descriptive words I learned to use
Accountability and responsibility
Manifestations I had to choose

My confidence soared in change

You would inherit my energy
Transferred directly to you from me
As I read, sang, and spoke
Sweet attributes, your spirit to free

I pursued change for you
I demanded change for me

My body shifted as you grew
No longer the body that I knew
My hips grew wider
My breast, heavy and thick
My hair grew longer
My gait, not as quick

No Rhyme or Reason, Just Thoughts for the Season

I watched my body change

Three weeks early
You declared it was time
Ready to show your beautiful face
I couldn't believe you were mine

My internal tempo refined
Moving to a different beat
Every fiber in me knew you were here
I finally felt complete

My heart even changed

I watched you grow
As the school years passed
Kissed wounds, did homework
Consoled breakups, and girl-friend clashes

I never knew I could be so protective
Like a child saying "MINE" to her toys
But putting it into perspective
You were always my greatest joy

We both grew and changed

You are an adult now
Flourishing and thriving at life
Celebrating successes
Navigating strife

Now I'm on the outskirts
Gently looking in
Watching as you blossom
When you need it, I freely lend a hand

Falling back is a new change

And now you have good news
Your own baby inside is growing
I picture my new grandbaby
Even though you are not showing

A Grandmom, what a joy
A girl, or a boy?
It matters not to me
I'll love you so deeply

What a joyful change

I look at my daughter
Her hips getting wide
Speaking differently about life
Walks with a distinctive stride

She plans
She plots
She thinks a lot
On the kind of Mother she will be

Deliberates
Contemplates
Meditates
On her life, what she foresees

Her goals
Her roles
Will all evolve
Around you; I see her grin

The transformation
The chapter of being a Mom
Starts deep within
…and so the change begins

No Rhyme or Reason, Just Thoughts for the Season

Her energy and
Adoration
Thanking her God above
For this change she feels
True love, fulfilled
For this little human
Unknown yet completely loved.

What a welcomed change.

Legacy

That lingering smell of cologne or perfume
When someone enters or leaves a room
Not too strong...you know, it's just right
Enough to make you notice and look beside

Who made that imprint
That gentle touch
That slight motion
Little nudge

That made you stand up tall
Look around
Smooth the wrinkles on you outfit down

Was it you?
Was it she or he?
That lingering smell, much like what we call
LEGACY

It's what we leave behind
That **impact** on your **soul**
Our **lineage**, our **children**
More precious than **Diamonds or Gold**

As you turn around and look
For that wafting smell, that delicacy
Don't forget to look inside
It may be you... leaving traces of your **LEGACY!**

Dare to Be the Legacy they dreamt you would be

Stolen

My lips
My hips
My butt
So what?

You think I don't see
All the things you have taken from me?

While I'm on my quest to be

Just Me

My dashiki

Colors so bright
Depicting my story
My ancestral right

Why do you wear
This stolen cloth
Does it represent
Your story or something you've lost?

No, it does not!!
My lips
My hips
My butt
My hair

Botox and braids are everywhere
My dance
My stance
How I look in my pants
Butt pads or injections

No Rhyme or Reason, Just Thoughts for the Season

You really give it a chance

Now you steal our very lives
You just breeze in
With no reason

Supported by fatalism
And
Systemic Racism
To cover up your facts
Your tracks
What you've stolen
I want back

My music
My song
The way I march on
I look how I look naturally
Not like you, because you stole from me.

What Say You? A story of legality

THE JUDGE

*I d*ecree
You were wrong

You know it
So here is your fine

There has to be a punishment
One that's suitable
For your crime

This is my job
You've crossed the line

Are you listening to me?

What say you, Sir
I am the Judge

What is your plea?

THE CRIMINAL

Plea?

Of course
I hear your every word

No desire
To act like
Your words
Are not heard

No Rhyme or Reason, Just Thoughts for the Season

I was not right
Rolling deep
In muck
And in mire

There is no excuse
I'm a criminal
Please
Just don't bring the fire

What say you?

THE WRONGED:

YOU
Took from me
Stole more than "things"

I want out of my skin
Escape the pain this brings

I trusted you
Welcomed you into my home

How dare you
Turn...
And do me wrong

I am the victim
The Broken

In total despair

What say you?
Jury

Do you even care?

THE JURY

CARE?

Yes
We care
That's part of the role

We have feelings
They help

Balance this heavy
Mental load

It's required
When weighing
Wrong from right

It's hard
Rendering justice

In this
We take no delight

However
Comma

Yes, the punctuation
I spelled out

There is a criminal
There is a victim

That is what these proceedings are about

And while we want to rest easy
Lying in our beds at night

No Rhyme or Reason, Just Thoughts for the Season

The goal is really to do the right thing
Yes, we want to get this right

In weighing all the evidence
Before we render our decree

Know that we DO care

We 12, on the jury

THE DECISION:

Can you imagine
Doing this

Day in
Day out
Mercy
Grace
Justice
Respect

We toss those words about

The expectations
Of all
This debate

The decision

By Judge and Jury

For something possibly committed by the criminal
Against the wronged, against the victim to some degree

Fate is shoveled out
Exponentially

Demetra "Lyrically" Adams

Emotions
Trauma
Forgiveness

Unforgiveness

The decision hangs in the air

The verdict:

We the jury
I, the Judge

Find you....

Yes, you heard it.
Do you think the verdict was fair?

What say you?

No Rhyme or Reason, Just Thoughts for the Season

No Rhyme or Reason, Just Thoughts for the Season

PAIN

You search for me in the middle of the night
I recognize your touch
And that is to your sheer delight

It starts slow
Usually left side of my face
Left eye
Softly weaving circles and designs around like fine lace
Intermittent stabbing…jabbing

Penetrating
I awaken
Shaken

Questioning
Contemplating
Why must daily, we partake in

This intrigue
Thinking
We are closer than we actually are

You pretend
You must believe
That we are friends
We are not friends

You keep me safe
No qualms admitting that
We are also not enemies
This is true, it is a fact

Demetra "Lyrically" Adams

My mind is spinning
You're pulling me closer
Not in an erotic way
And yet full of possession
I belong to you today

You are intentional
In how you make me feel
You are deliberate
On this day, one of many that you steal

You expect a response
And to not respond garners an even deeper touch
You will not let go, until you make me
Give some response up...
But I've grown tough

I hold out as long as I can
But eventually
As you know will happen
I can no longer withstand

A deep moan
I tighten my eyes
Anger emerges as I envision you smirk
I groan
You got what you wanted
My body was just on loan

I wince
Relief floods through me
You got your response
So now you withdrew
You've set me free

You never stop completely
Silent tears fall as you loosen your hold
Feeling as though my will has been broken
Since you've entered my life, do I ever have control?

No Rhyme or Reason, Just Thoughts for the Season

Not unlike being physically raped
I, unfortunately, can speak to this comparison first hand

Pain
A constant passenger taking over,
An abusive lover having their way,
Whenever…
Over, and over
Again, and again.

Pain,
You searched for me in the night

Pain,
You found me

Pain,
You left me empty
Barren
Spent
Lonely
Sad

Knowing you will return
When you see fit
And I am trapped

Pain.

Demetra "Lyrically" Adams

Who Am I? (In Memory 05/25/2020)

These are the facts
What we typically see
In the childhood
Of a Black that we feel will not succeed

Of one walking the streets
Causing trouble, a plenty
Hustling for food, clothes
Rent, for every penny

Parents divorced
Changing schools all the time
A blended face in the crowd
Never any conversation…never anything kind

He finally grows up
Gets a job
No one wants to work by his side
He ends up with all the newbies
Teaching them how to toe the line

Complaints pile up, 18 in 19 years
Slipping under the radar
Step to him, no one dares

He is not Black
And he's a body that fills a spot

Who cares if he is
An angry, White cop

What can go wrong
Just keep him on staff
Even his co-workers
Don't put him in check

No Rhyme or Reason, Just Thoughts for the Season

When you have a lit bomb
And you feed it oxygen
One day
He may put his knee on someone's neck.

Mirror, Mirror (In Memory 01/07/2023)

I get up in the morning
Smile on my face
Camera in hand
Headed to my favorite place

I love going to the skate park
Skateboarding since I was six
Hoping when my son is older
He will also like to do this

Mirror, mirror
On the wall
Capturing photographs
As nighttime falls

All the beauty
Sun going to bed
Colors blend
Orange and Red

Watching the sunset
Peace…nothing to dread

No way of knowing
I would soon be dead

I get up in the morning
Put on my uniform
Shine my Badge
Get my gun

No Rhyme or Reason, Just Thoughts for the Season

A group of cops
Scorpion is the name
Tightknit justice
Dishing it out
No shame in their game

Mirror, mirror
On the wall
A group of Black cops
One and all

Aware of racism
Permeating
Systemically

Escalating
Prolifically

Are you feeling me?
Hearing me?
This shit is reeling me...

Mirror, Mirror
Did you see
The skater in the car
That just drove down the street?

Society is peeping hard
No violation can we see

Check your mirror, mirror
For severity?

Check it, mirror, mirror
What was the degree
For this penalty?

Scorpion beat this young man senseless
We demand to know what his offense was?

What image did the mirror, mirror
On your wall
See as this young man's fatal flaw?

You forgot he was a brother?
Black, like you
Black like me?

Before I catch this heat
Of people saying
For Black crime
A pass, I want to see

That is not what I'm saying
It's not true
Just let me speak

It's justice
That I seek
Ultimately

Let the punishment
Fit the crime

It shouldn't be DEATH
Every
Single
Damn
Time

Justice
For the laws we break
For lives we take
For rules we disobey

No Rhyme or Reason, Just Thoughts for the Season

Not finality
Stop killing me
Because my Black skin
Displeases
Your sensibilities

Justice
Not death
They are NOT one and the same

Because you wear that badge
Why should my punishment surpass
That of any other ethnic or racial class?

Did you think we would not ask?

I pray for consistency
In treatment
Regardless of ethnicity or race
My mirror, mirror would like to know
What you saw that day?

You brought shame to your community
Dishonor to your race
Black police
Killing their own
That is the epitome of disgrace

Mirror, mirror
On the wall

You are the police
Not Judge…Jury

You are not
God!

As a matter of fact
You've lost your damn mind

Demetra "Lyrically" Adams

I know you are ready
For me to stop this rhyme

I'm taking my time....
You took your time

Now there you are
Beating this stranger
A skater
A photographer
A father
A son

While someone was out there
Shooting, killing, beating, robbing someone

Mirror, mirror
On the wall

She won't forget this day at all

They came to her door
Said her son she could not see

He was somewhere close
But no one implied
That they had beaten him unmercifully

She did not know
Until the doctor called

That the mirror to her soul
Her son
Lay in critical condition
She was appalled

Bless you, Mother.

No Rhyme or Reason, Just Thoughts for the Season

My final words
To those who took her son away

Every time you look
In the mirror, mirror
Shame…shame
I pray, you feel all over your cruel face.

To his precious Mother
Peace, I pray for you
Not as the world gives…

You said your son was sent here for a mission
A purpose
And now his work is done.

That beautiful smile
Exists in the presence
Of the Most Holy One.

Heading towards Loss

Thank You, Heavenly Father
For all that You've given to me
For grace, Mercy
Don't forget about Joy
Which is my strength in time of need

As I'm faced with the impending loss
Of someone great in my life
I still want to thank You
For being with me tonight

I feel Your comfort
I rest in Your peace
I know my Father
Will soon be released

From any earthly pain
From the attachment to that bed
From the inability to say what he wants
To get his thoughts out of his head

You're a good God, Jesus
Of course, some may differ at times like these

But that's only because they see the loss
But I see the upcoming victory

Dad, you will run and jump and praise the Lord
Heaven will no longer be a mystery

You fought wars here that were not your own
For those, you suffered endlessly

No Rhyme or Reason, Just Thoughts for the Season

Now your earthly battle is almost over
My entire body aches are the mere thought
I know I'm headed to tell you good-bye
But really, I'm just seeing you off. *I'll see you again Dad. I love you.*

Demetra "Lyrically" Adams

The Day the Mountain Fell

Dedicated to Mr. Willie G. Adams I aka Dad 06/25/2022

The mountain stands so tall
Arrogant and all
Wonderful to watch
Zest for life, his smile says it all

Vietnam Vet
The Army took him young
Had the gall to send him
Not once, twice but three times
To a war that was not his own

After the war left him raw
The bottle became his best friend
His marriage came to an end
Damage soon began

But wait, hold up
Don't judge my Dad
Vietnam gave him a disease that attacked his liver
All the facts, make certain you have

The mountain now has different shapes
The winds of life take its toll
There have been children
Walking up and down the mountain
Leaving marks with their soles in his soul

Here I am
Watching my father
This mountain so tall to me
Come in and out of my life
I wanted to please him

No Rhyme or Reason, Just Thoughts for the Season

However, in my youth, he was an absentee
In my older years
This mega man
Has been a fierce and huge part of my life
I'm so glad we reconciled
I thank God for healing our strife

I am grateful for the many years
We had together to share
Laughter
Poker
Singing
Silence

The mountain was always there

He has not let me do without
His presence
A birthday song
He has not let me do without
Advice
Discerning right from wrong

I thank God for giving to me
The relationship that I've have with my Dad
For making up for past mistakes
For giving the good and the bad

It gave me a perspective
Of this man
This mountainous man that I see
Of just how huge
His heart really is
Of how much he has always loved me.

We all have perspectives
Conjured or contrived
About how people's lives should have been lived
How the mountain should have been in our lives

Demetra "Lyrically" Adams

So now, the mountain has fallen
And I don't know what to do
I see the crumbles
My heart is breaking
Jesus, I'm calling You

I hear you when you pray, Sweetheart
Please, calm your mind and soul
My ways confound the wise
This mountain shall not be stole

Though you see it getting smaller each day
It is not as it seems
The mountain is being lifted upwards
I'm bringing your Dad home to Me

He has fought enough battles
The emotional wars here on this earth are done
He has loved his children, each and every one

He has so many friends
Too many to count
And brothers who fought beside

But it's time My sweet
His battle is complete
He's coming to the other side

I'm lifting the mountain up
Slowly everyday
I did not want, too quickly
To take your Dad away
But please don't be deceived
When his stature, his mountainous being, you see decline
He is not falling, crumbling, or broken

He's just being pulled upward
Because, your Dad, he is Mine.

No Rhyme or Reason, Just Thoughts for the Season

Celebrating your homegoing, to be with the Lord. I love you Dad.

Epilogue

Thank You for Reading

Thank you so much for reading this poetic book of feelings and emotions that captured this author's feelings from 2019-2023.

A dynamic time in history with the pandemic, racial tension, and Black Lives Matter, pain has been palpable and tears have been abundant. Lyric takes to the pen to release and reveal her pain, anger, and search for healing.

Some might say my words are spoken from a bitter heart. I am not bitter.
Some might say I live in the past. I am extremely present and forward thinking.

The reality of this book is that it speaks truth. It may not be your truth but it is capital "T" the Truth. These things happened. They still happen. Believe it, accept it or choose not to, that does not change the Truth.

I appreciate all comments, positive and negative. Comments mean we are having conversations about uncomfortable topics. Conversations, though there may stir friction, bring about change.

Thank you for the Words

Though the thanks
Congrats
The accolades

These may come to me

The praise, Dear Lord
Will always go to You
For what people read

I know these words
And all the words
Written historically

Have come from You
Dearest Lord
You gave them all to me

As I close this book
This book of poetry

I lift my hands
My heart
My soul
Giving thanks for every word I see

I am just a vessel
We co-create
You and me

I pick up the pen
You whisper the words
Albeit
Some mixed with my humanity

No Rhyme or Reason, Just Thoughts for the Season

It's time to close this chapter now
This book is certainly complete
I pray it touches many hearts
Makes some fall to their knees

Convict
Convince
Make many confess
If they know they have been described

By the words
The words You've given to me
Written down, here inside.

Thank You, Dear Lord, for every word. Amen.

About the Author

Demetra "Lyrically" Adams

In her first poetry book "No Reason or Rhyme, just thoughts over Time" Adams showcased poems written from her high school years to mid-thirties. In this long-awaited follow-up, "No Rhyme or Reason – just Thoughts for the Season", Lyric actually takes current events and responds with words that many of us only wished we could conjure. Lyric does admit, her style, and her words, may not be for everyone; however, she speaks them because they are her truth.

Demetra "Lyrically" Adams is a veteran of the US Air Force, an entrepreneur, registered nurse, and certified professional coach and case manager. She prides herself on being a positive contributor to society; moving, weaving, and leaving her mark for future generations to follow.

Contact the Author: Lyric@HYRProductions.com

"I do not write because I like to; I write because I HAVE to." I believe words have the power to both give and to take life. Use them cautiously because once they are set free...they become like ripples of current in water; you never know the vast affect they will have or when they will finally stop moving.." Lyric

www.ingramcontent.com/pod-product-compliance
Lightning Source LLC
Chambersburg PA
CBHW070051120426
42742CB00048B/2395